"We have a *promise* we can count on, because we have a *Promiser* who has never failed and can never fail."

A. W. Tozer

THIS BOOK BELONGS TO _____

Published by Christian Art Publishers
PO Box 1599, Vereeniging, 1930, RSA

© 2021
First edition 2021

Designed by Christian Art Publishers

Cover designed by Christian Art Publishers
Images used under license from Shutterstock.com

Printed in China

ISBN 978-1-4321-3478-5

22 23 24 25 26 27 28 29 30 31 – 13 12 11 10 9 8 7 6 5 4

Color
– the –
PROMISES
of GOD

**CHRISTIAN ART
PUBLISHERS**

"FOR THE
MOUNTAINS MAY MOVE AND
THE HILLS DISAPPEAR,
BUT EVEN THEN MY FAITHFUL LOVE
FOR YOU WILL REMAIN. MY COVENANT OF
BLESSING WILL NEVER BE BROKEN,"
SAYS THE LORD.

ISAIAH 54:10

"Look at the *birds* of the air; they do not *sow* or *reap* or *store away* in barns, and yet your *heavenly Father* feeds them. Are you not much *more valuable* than they?"

MATTHEW 6:26

"I am the light of the world. If you follow Me, you won't have to walk in darkness, because you will have the light that leads to life."

John 8:12

"FOR I KNOW THE PLANS I HAVE FOR YOU," declares the Lord "PLANS TO PROSPER YOU & NOT TO HARM YOU, PLANS TO GIVE YOU hope AND A future."

JEREMIAH 29:11

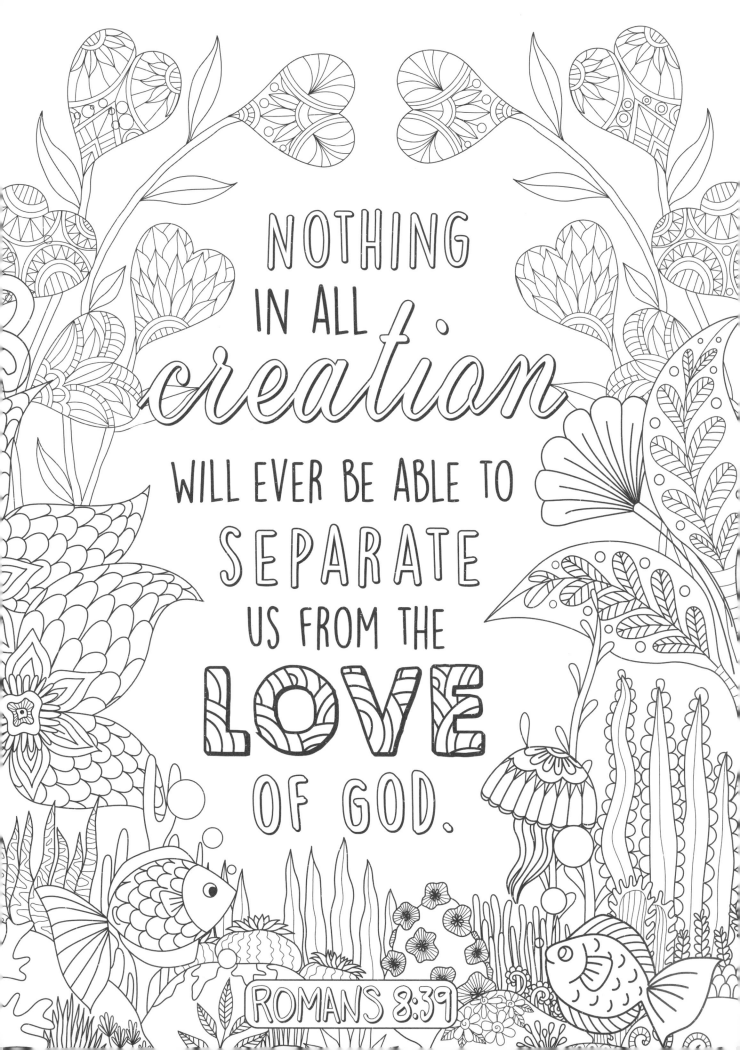

"I HAVE COME THAT THEY MAY HAVE LIFE, AND THAT THEY MAY HAVE IT MORE ABUNDANTLY."

JOHN 10:10

Blessed are those who trust in the LORD & have made the LORD their hope & confidence.

Jeremiah 17:7

"WHEN YOU PASS THROUGH THE *waters,* I WILL BE WITH *you.* WHEN YOU CROSS RIVERS, YOU WILL NOT DROWN."

ISAIAH 43:2

We have this
HOPE
as an
anchor
for the
soul

Hebrews 6:19

THE LORD IS MY shepherd; I HAVE ALL THAT I need.

Psalm 23:1

"Come to Me,
ALL WHO LABOR AND ARE
HEAVY LADEN,
AND I WILL GIVE YOU rest."

MATTHEW 11:28

The *Joy* OF THE LORD IS YOUR *Strength!*

NEHEMIAH 8:10

OVERWHELMING
VICTORY
IS OURS THROUGH CHRIST,
WHO LOVED US.
ROMANS 8:37

YOUR WORD IS A LAMP TO MY FEET AND A *light* TO MY PATH.

Psalm 119:105

Because of
God's
tender mercy,
the morning light from heaven
is about to break upon us.

LUKE 1:78

The
LORD will be
your *everlasting*
light.
Isaiah 60:20

"I AM the Vine; YOU ARE THE branches. If you remain in ME AND I IN YOU, you will bear much fruit." ~ John 15:5

Give thanks to the LORD, for He is good! His faithful LOVE endures forever. PSALM 118:29

"Be still & know that I am God."

Psalm 46:10

The name of the
LORD IS A strong tower;
THE RIGHTEOUS
RUN TO IT
AND ARE
safe.

Proverbs 18:10

THE faithful LOVE of the LORD never ends! His mercies never cease.

Lamentations 3:22

Jesus Christ is the same Yesterday, today & forever.

Hebrews 13:8

The
eternal God
is your refuge,
and underneath are the
everlasting
arms.

Deuteronomy
- 33:27 -

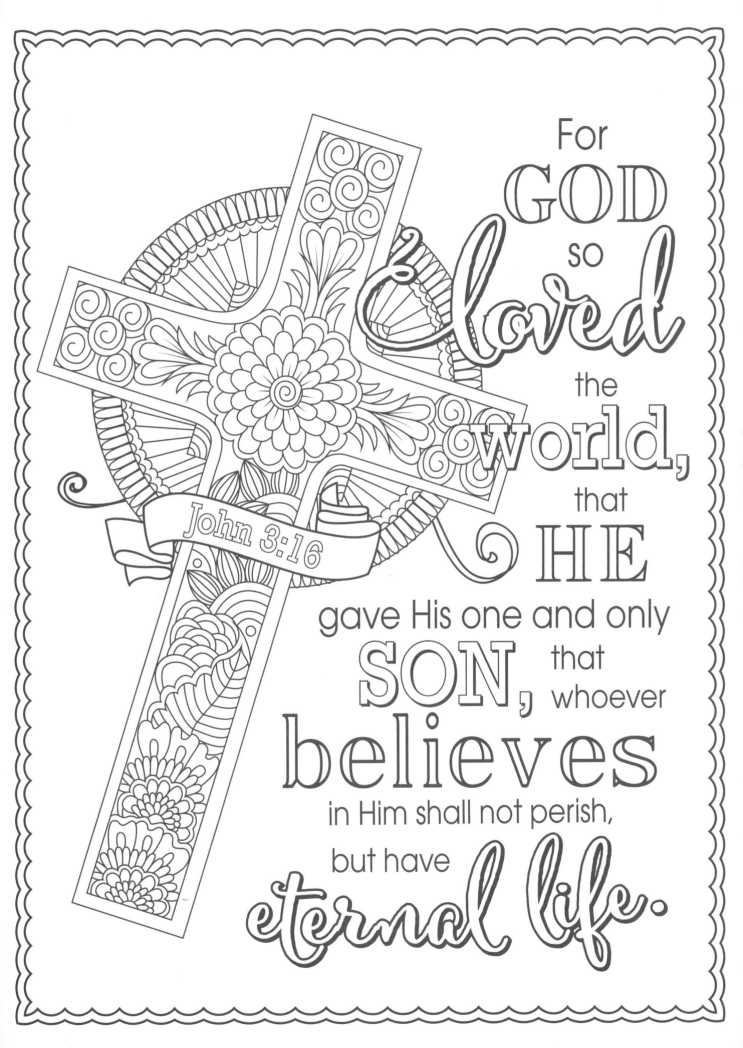

For GOD so loved the world, that HE gave His one and only SON, that whoever believes in Him shall not perish, but have eternal life.

John 3:16

This is God, our God forever and ever. He will guide us forever. Psalm 48:14

Great is HIS faithfulness; HIS mercies begin afresh each morning.

Lamentations 3:23

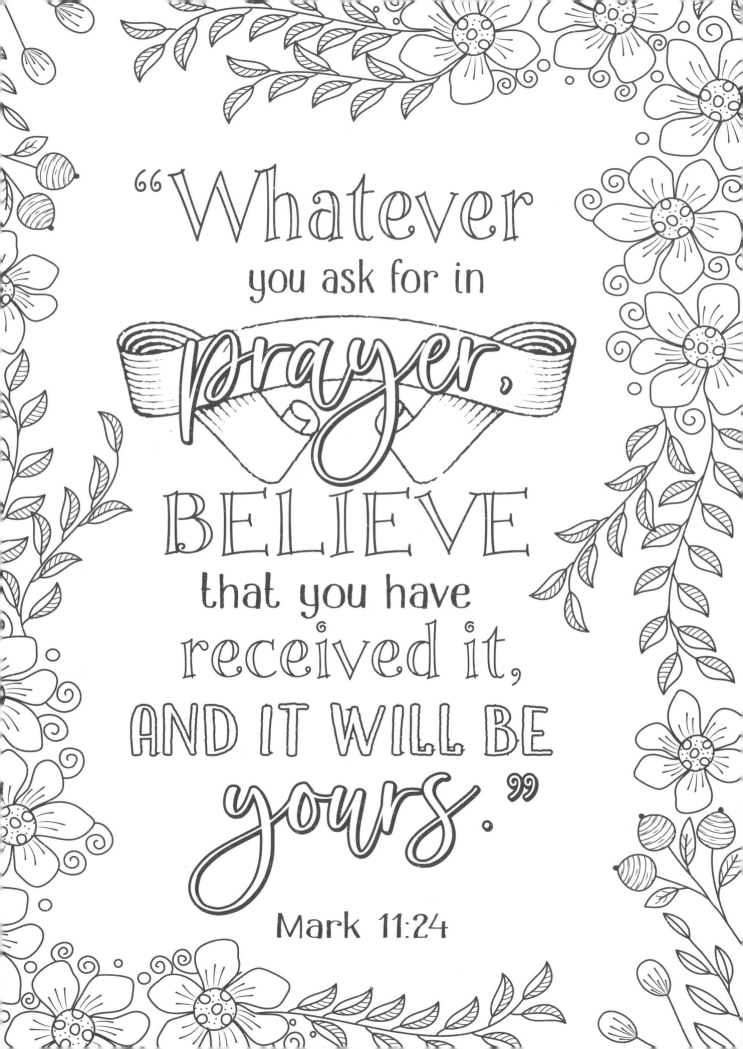

"Whatever you ask for in *Prayer*, BELIEVE that you have received it, AND IT WILL BE *yours*."

Mark 11:24

The
LORD
is good,

a stronghold   in the day of trouble;
and He knows those who
TRUST IN HIM.

Nahum 1:7

Take delight in the Lord, and HE will give you your heart's desires.

Psalm 37:4

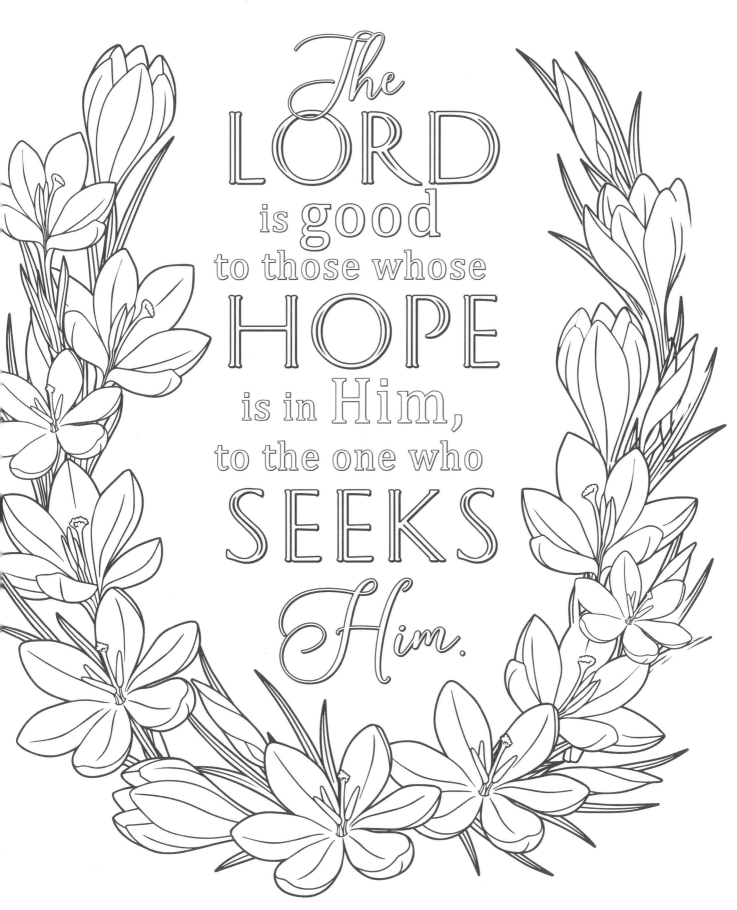

The LORD is good to those whose HOPE is in Him, to the one who SEEKS Him.

LAMENTATIONS 3:25

"So I say to you, ask, and it will be given to you; seek, and you will find; knock, and it will be opened to you."

Luke 11:9

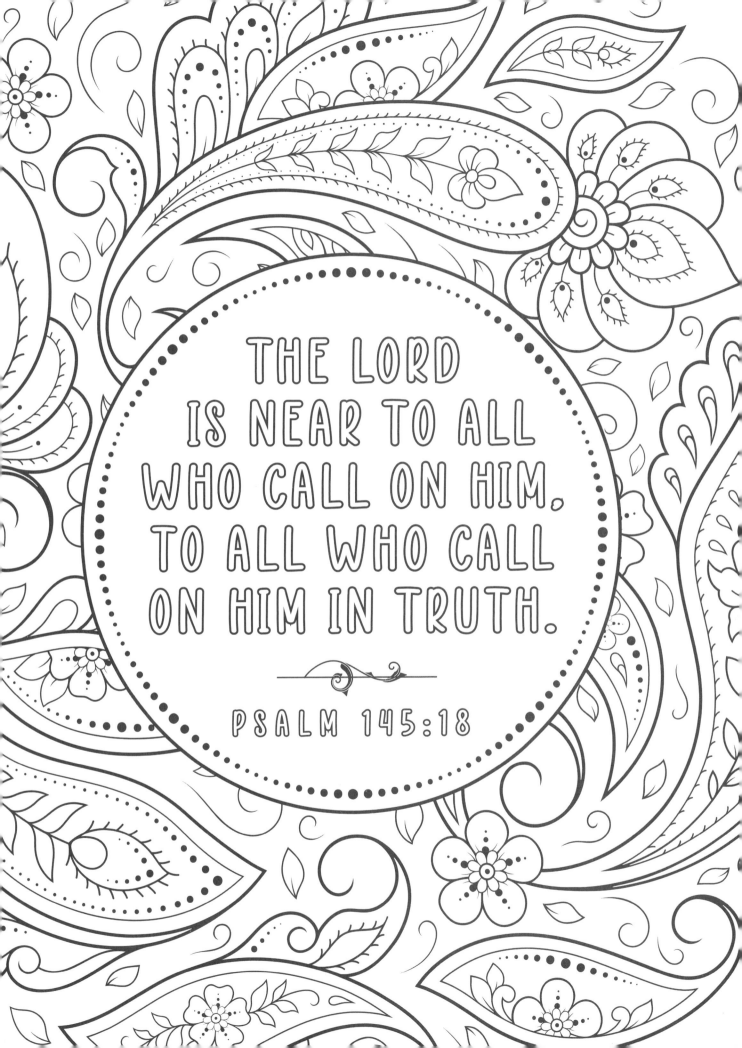

"The LORD will fight for you; you need only to be still."

Exodus 14:14

GOD IS OUR refuge AND STRENGTH, A VERY PRESENT help IN TROUBLE.

PSALM 46:1

Give thanks TO THE LORD for He is good

JESUS CHRIST IS THE SAME YESTERDAY, TODAY & FOREVER.

HEBREWS 13:8

Give all your worries & cares to God, for HE CARES about you.

1 Peter 5:7

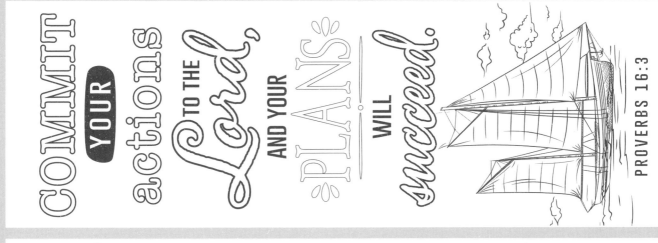

COMMIT YOUR actions TO THE Lord, AND YOUR PLANS WILL succeed.

PROVERBS 16:3

NOTHING IN ALL creation WILL EVER BE ABLE TO SEPARATE US FROM THE LOVE OF GOD.

ROMANS 8:39

Our God WILL guide us Forever. PSALM 48:14

THE FAITHFUL love OF THE LORD NEVER ends!

LAMENTATIONS 3:22

FOLD

FOLD

FOLD

Psalm 118:24

Today is the day
the Lord has made!

God
loves
you!

May
the Lord
bless &
keep
you.

FOLD

NEHEMIAH 8:10

The
JOY
OF THE
LORD
IS YOUR
Strength!

Colossians 1:11

May you
be filled with

FOLD

Numbers 6:24

I pray that God will
greatly bless you with kindness,
peace, and love!

Jude 2

FOLD